FASHION

ANNE SCHRAFF

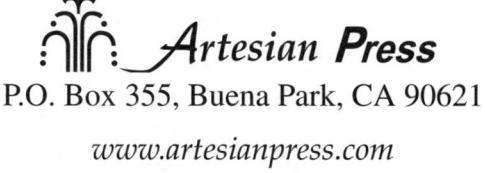

P.O. Box 355, Buena Park, CA 90621

www.artesianpress.com

Nonfiction
eXtreme Customs Series

Cover image of Louis XIV period woman's hat
Editor: Zac Miller
Graphic Design: Tony Amaro
©2006 Artesian Press

www.artesianpress.com

 *Artesian* **Press**   ISBN 1-58659-213-0

Contents

Word List

accessories (ak-SES-eh-reez) Things worn with an outfit to make a complete look, such as belts, jewelry, scarves, and hats.

archeologist (ark-ee-AHL-uh-jist) A scientist who tries to find the truth about things that happened in the past.

Assyria (uh-SEER-ee-uh) An ancient empire of western Asia.

brocade (broh-KADE) An oriental silk fabric with a raised pattern of gold and silver.

brooches (BROO-chez) Pieces of jewelry that are held by pins or clasps and usually worn near the neck.

carmine (KAR-mine) A dye made from the dried bodies of insects.

chador (CHEH-der) A large cloth usually worn by Muslim women as a combination head covering, veil, and shawl.

chopines (chah-PEENS) Brocaded leather slippers attached to wooden stilts about two feet high.

crinoline (KRIN-uh-lin) An open-weave fabric of horsehair or cotton that is stiffened and used for underskirts and lining.

cuticles (KYEW-ti-kulz) The skin around each fingernail.

damask (DA-mesk) A fabric that is a bit stiff and shiny and has flat patterns.

dhoti (DOE-tee) A kind of loincloth worn by men in India.

embroidered (em-BROY-derd) Having fancy patterns made with needlework.

ermine (ER-min) An animal like a weasel whose fur turns white in winter and is used to make fur coats and trim.

Euphrates (yoo-FRATE-eez) A large Middle Eastern river that flows through Turkey and Iraq, where it joins the Tigris River.

farthingale (FAR-then-gale) A kind of support, formed of hoops, worn under a skirt to make it wider at the hips.

henna (HEH-nuh) A reddish-brown dye made from a plant and usually put in hair.

kimono (kee-MOE-noh) A loose robe tied at the waist with a sash.

palla (PAH-luh) A cloaklike garment sometimes worn over a toga.

Papua New Guinea (PA-pyew-eh noo GIN-ee) An island country in the western Pacific Ocean.

Pima (PEE-muh) Native Americans who lived in the southwestern United States (Arizona).

pleated (PLEE-ted) A garment that has many folds of cloth made by doubling the material over on itself.

Papago (puh-PAY-go) Native Americans who lived in the southwestern United States (Arizona).

saffron (SAF-ron) Dried parts of crocus flowers used to dye or color things yellow.

sari (SAH-ree) A long piece of cloth that is usually framed on three sides by decorations of flowering plants and abstract symbols.

sarong (seh-RONG) A traditional wrap-around skirt worn by people in Indonesia.

Sumerians (suh-MARE-ee-enz) People who lived between the Tigris and Euphrates rivers.

tapa (TAH-peh) A cloth made by beating, drying, and decorating the inner bark of the mulberry tree.

ti (tee) Leaves on certain trees or shrubs that grow in Asia and the Pacific islands.

Tigris (TIE-gris) A river that flows through Turkey and Iraq where it joins the Euphrates River.

toga (TOE-guh) A garment made from a sheet of cloth about 9 yards long and draped attractively around the body.

tunic (TOO-nik) A simple slip-on garment with or without sleeves, usually knee length, belted at the waist.

turban (TER-bun) A headdress made of a cap with a long cloth wound around it, worn mostly in Mediterranean and Middle Eastern countries.

Yoruba (yoe-ROO-buh) A tribe living in Nigeria, Africa.

yucca (YUK-uh) A plant with spiny leaves that grows in warm climates.

Chapter 1

Everybody Wears Something

Imagine a very well-dressed gentleman wearing a wide-brimmed hat decorated with loops of striped green ribbon. Hanging from under his hat he has long corkscrew curls that reach his shoulders. His red coat is knee length. His pants are also knee length and are tied with ribbons. His stockings are tight, and his shoes have high heels. In Europe in the 1600s, he was wearing the latest fashions.

At the very same time in Papua New Guinea (PA-pyew-eh noo GIN-ee), in the western Pacific Ocean, a proud man is wearing decorations made from clay, wood, and shells on his arms and legs. On his head is a huge headdress made from the colorful feathers of a bird of paradise. His skirtlike costume is made from the feathers of the white cockatoo and black cassowary birds.

9

In his village, he is known as a snappy dresser.

What people wore at any time in history depended a lot on where they lived. How much or how little they wore depended a great deal on the weather. The Native Americans in California wore a piece of material that hung from the waist in the front and back. It was called a breech cloth. When the weather got cold, they put on cloaks made from rabbit or deerskin. Native American women wore grass skirts or leather aprons. They also wore cloaks in the cold weather. Their cloaks were sometimes made from otter or wildcat skins.

Native Americans wore simple clothing, but they still thought about how they looked. They decorated their hair with small shells, bones, and stones. They also wore fancy headdresses made of feathers and beads.

The Pima (PEE-muh) and Papago (puh-PAY-go) people who lived in the southwest United States were good weavers. They

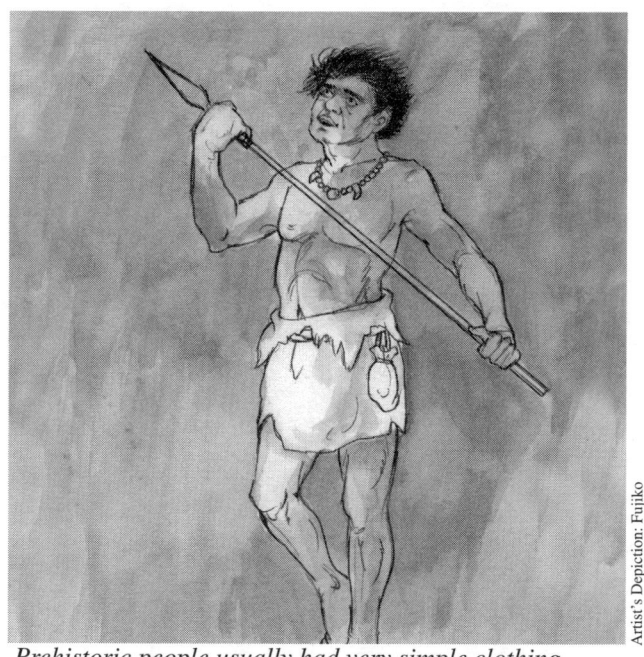

Prehistoric people usually had very simple clothing.

used yucca (YUK-uh), bear grass, and other natural materials to weave mats, bags, and baskets. The men wore yucca sandals and deerskin clothing that wrapped around their bodies. The women wore woven tunics (TOO-niks).

There were two reasons why early people wore clothes. They wore them mainly for protection against bad weather. They also liked to decorate themselves. They most likely got the idea when they noticed that many animals and birds had fur and feathers to keep them warm. So cave dwellers wrapped themselves in the skins and furs of bison, tigers, mammoths, reindeer, gorillas, and wolves. People today use a process called tanning to make animal hides soft and wearable, but cave people had to invent their own ways of keeping the skins from becoming hard when they dried out. They soaked the hides in water, beat them with huge hammers, and even chewed them to make them soft. Cave dwellers wrapped strips of these softened animal hides around their feet, making the very first shoes. Sometimes these early people colored the hides with powered red, yellow, or black rocks.

Chapter 2

The First Fashions

An Egyptian woman wearing pleated clothes.

At some point around 12,000 years ago, cloth replaced hide in some places. The Ancient Egyptians wove cloth from flax and cotton, but it came apart easily. So the people began draping their clothes around their bodies and tying them at the waist to keep them in place.

Needles that could be threaded were invented, and the first true fabrics became common. Soon afterwards, the loom was invented, and that made weaving garments easier and faster.

In ancient Egypt, clothes were almost

always white, but once in a while colorful thread was sewn into the garments in pretty designs. The clothing was draped and pleated (PLEE-ted). It was important to the Egyptians to be in style and to look beautiful. Cleanliness was important, and people took baths often. Hair was styled with combs and hairpins. Barbers often came to the homes of rich women to help them style their hair. Some men and women shaved their heads so they could wear wigs made from the hair of slaves or sheep's wool. They used beeswax to glue the wigs to their bald heads. Wigs were blue, green, blond, or gold. People decorated them with gold dust or golden beads.

Makeup was easy to get in Egypt if you were rich. Women used rosewater and egg whites for facials. They spread perfumed oil on their skin and used yellow-red henna (HEH-nuh) dye on their nails. Lips were colored orange-red with carmine dye (KAR-mine), made from dried insect bodies. Nothing was colored bright red in

Egypt because the people thought that color was magical or even dangerous. People who had red hair were thought of as freaks. Veins on the forehead were colored with blue dye so you could see them better. The Egyptians thought that this was beautiful. Crushed ant eggs were used to outline the eyes. Eyelids were colored green or black, and there were beauty secrets for women with skin problems.

Blemishes, or pimples, could be cleared up by putting on a cream made from a young bull's bile, which is the yellow liquid that comes from the liver. Whipped ostrich eggs, dough, and milk were also used to clear up skin. To get rid of wrinkles, women made a potion out of incense, olive oil, and wax and spread it on their faces. This potion had to stay on the face for six full days in order to work.

Chapter 3

Fashions from 6,000 to 1,000
Years Ago

About 6,000 years ago, people called Sumerians (suh-MARE-ee-enz) lived along the banks of the Tigris (TIE-gris) and Euphrates (yoo-FRATE-eez) rivers, which flow through parts of the Middle East. Sumerian women wore their hair in heavy rolls and braids. They powdered it with gold dust or perfumed yellow starch. They also wore gold hairpins. Sumerian men dyed their hair and beards black and shaped them with curling irons.

Sumerians wore woolen clothing, often fringed shawls. They invented tweezers for pulling out unwanted hair, toothpicks to help keep their teeth clean, and bone instruments used to push back cuticles (KYEW-ti-kulz) on the fingers to make their hands more attractive.

For the ancient Greeks, the palla (PAH-luh) was the most common outer garment. It was fastened at the shoulders, leaving the arms bare. A belt was used to hold it at the waist. Each morning, Greek women covered their entire bodies with perfumes and ointments. Then they washed their hair and added powders, colored black, sky blue, or gold. They painted their eyebrows black and curled their hair with hot irons.

Greek men of this time wore tunics that were belted just below the chest. To protect themselves against the sun, they wore cone-shaped hats with a narrow brim. The Greeks usually went barefoot, except in the cooler weather. Then they wore sandals. The soles of their sandals had studs in them, like some of the winter tires we put on our cars, so they wouldn't slip in bad weather.

Ancient Romans wore a piece of clothing called a toga (TOE-guh.) A toga was a sheet of cloth, usually white, about nine yards long. It was draped attractively around

A man in a toga

the body, however it was not comfortable. Most Romans changed to tunics, which looked like long T-shirts. Togas and tunics were made of wool, and the rich decorated the edges with color. Pins or brooches (BROO-chez) were used to hold the clothing together. Roman men did not wear pants until their armies began invading colder lands. Both men and women wore sandals on their feet.

Like other ancient people, Romans wanted to look beautiful. Men dusted their hair with colored powder or gold dust. Women used yellow soap to make their hair blond. Sometimes they wore wigs made from the blond hair of prisoners taken in war. Makeup included wood ash and saffron (SAF-ron) to color the skin around their eyes and blue paint to outline veins.

Meal paste and lemon juice were used to make freckles disappear. Rich Roman women used ivory combs. Poor women used combs made of bone. Some people say that the real purpose of combs in Rome was to get rid of lice, not to style hair.

It was popular to have very pale skin in Rome, so women used powdered chalk or white lead to cover the skin of their faces. The only mirrors at that time were pieces of highly polished metal. Some people spent hours looking at themselves.

Jewelry was popular, and many people wore it. Women wore fancy gold pieces and pearls on their necks and arms. They also wore rings on their fingers and pretty pins on their clothing.

In Middle Eastern countries, women often kept their hair covered with a hood. Many people believed that a woman needed to cover her hair to be modest.

About 1,000 years ago, some Europeans traveled to Turkey. There they discovered different kinds of clothing and new fabrics—

like cotton garments and Asian gowns, embroidered (em-BROY-derd) heavy silk and fabrics that had fancy patterns or jewel decorations.

European workers wore loose, simple garments so they could do their work easily. Rich Europeans, who did not do any hard work, made beautiful but clumsy clothing. For the first time in human history, artificial shapes—padding—were put into clothing. It was more important to look beautiful and be in style rather than to be comfortable.

Chapter 4

The Middle Ages in Europe
(A.D. 500–1500)

Women's clothing became elegant in the Middle Ages. They wore bright red robes that were decorated with fancy stitching and feathers. Silk, fine wool, and fur were the most popular materials. Women wore linen underwear, petticoats made of wool or otter fur, and a long-sleeved gown or dress. On top of all this, they wore a sleeveless coat, which had sleeves that could be attached if needed. The coats were purple and were lined with green or blue damask (DA-mesk) and trimmed with ermine (ER-min).

Women's clothing became so elegant about 800 years ago in France that King Philippe de Del made laws telling people what kind of clothing they could wear. The number of garments a person could wear depended on his or her class, or importance in society. Only people of the nobility could wear ermine furs. Wives of dukes, earls, and barons were allowed to have four new dresses each year. Knights and their ladies could have no more than two new robes a year. Ordinary French people could not wear gold or valuable stones.

Poor people wore shoes that were just leather pouches wrapped around the foot and tied at the ankle. Rich people wore shoes made from soft leather as well as silk and velvet decorated with pearls. As time went on, shoes got pointier and heels got higher.

By the mid-1500s, the famous Queen Catherine de Medici began to wear shoes with very high heels. People in Venice, Italy, designed the chopines (chah-PEENZ) which were brocaded (broh-KADE-ed) leather slippers attached to wooden stilts about 2 feet high. The Queen of Spain needed two servants to help her walk around on her chopines.

Men and women in the upper classes

wore their hair in loose curls. Women hung gold balls at the ends of their strands of hair. Rich women wore gold threads in their hair. People of the lower classes wore their hair short—at their chins or their shoulders—and undecorated.

A high forehead was considered beautiful, so women often shaved their foreheads to make their hairlines higher. Then they decorated their foreheads with headbands. They painted their faces with white flour. A kind of beauty cream was made from the brains of a male pig, crocodile glands, and wolf's blood. It was supposed to guarantee smooth skin.

The things that women wore on their heads became spectacular in the Middle Ages and later on in Europe. Hats began to have wide shapes with side attachments just above the ears that crowned the head. These big hats were decorated with a lot of gold and jewelry, and some had veils hung at the ends. The horned headdress, with two high horns that stood on top of the head, became popular. The butterfly headdress was made of a see-through material put over a wire V-shaped frame that had a dip in front. Along with the fabulous hats came gloves that were richly embroidered and heavy with jewels. Red and white roses were also popular as accessories (ak-SES-eh-reez).

England's Queen Elizabeth the First had three hundred dresses. She hung each of them on its own hook in a special room. From this custom came the idea of closets. The queen also had eighty wigs and twenty-seven fans. When she was young, the queen had curly red hair, and many women tried to look like her, using different ways to turn their own hair red. When their ideas didn't work, they wore red wigs. When she saw signs that she was growing old, Queen Elizabeth was so upset that she refused to look in a mirror for twenty years.

Even though she had elegant clothing of her own, Queen Elizabeth passed laws saying what other women could wear. For example, middle-class women could only

A picture of Anne of Cleves, the fourth wife of Henry VIII.

have velvet facings on their sleeves, while people of the nobility could wear full velvet sleeves.

About 600 years ago in Europe, it was popular for men to have fat stomachs that hung over their tightly belted waists. Men even used padding to make it look like they had big bellies.

Chapter 5

The Middle Ages Around the World

While Europeans were dressing in fancy velvets and wearing fantastic headwear, people in other parts of the world were dressing in much different ways. In lands that followed Islamic customs, women wore long black gowns called chadors (CHEH-derz) that covered their entire bodies. Buddhist monks in Thailand wore simple orange robes that looked like togas.

In New Zealand, clothing was made from seeds, leaves, grass, tree bark, shells, fur, feathers, and even sea creatures. In Papua New Guinea, the inner bark of the mulberry tree was beaten, dried, and decorated to make a cloth called tapa (TAH-peh). The tapa cloth was then made into a wraparound garment worn by men.

In the Solomon Islands in the Pacific Ocean, grass skirts were made with strips of

A Maori man in tribal dress.

banana leaves that had been dried in the sun. The strips were tied together at the waist. The leaves were sometimes dyed to make multicolored stripes. Hawaiians also made grass skirts using green ti (tee) leaves.

27

The people of northern Canada and Alaska wrapped themselves in furs from seals, polar bears, caribou, and fox. In the high Andes Mountains of Peru and Bolivia in South America, women wore several brightly colored cotton skirts on top of each other and a bright cotton shawl.

In India and Pakistan, poor people often decorated their clothing with the shiny wings of beetles, which glitter like jewelry. Both men and women in Indonesia wore, and still wear today, a sarong (seh-RONG), a cool, traditional wraparound skirt.

The people of Kenya, Africa, wore wraparound garments, beaded collars, and head-dresses. Palm trees were used in weaving garments in many parts of Africa. People of the Yoruba (yoe-ROO-buh) culture in Nigeria wore long wraparound clothing and turbans (TER-bunz) on their heads. Tie-dye patterns were popular there just as they have been in the United States since the 1960s. Tightly tying or stitching sections of cloth and then dipping the material into a mixture of colors create the patterns seen on tye-die clothing.

Men in northwestern Africa wore large black robes and baggy pants. In Ghana, craftsmen made brightly colored cloth and passed these skills on to their sons.

In Arab countries, where the weather is usually hot and loose, flowing clothes gave protection from the sun. Earth tones, such as green, blue, gray, brown, black, and white were preferred.

In China, patterns for garments were simple. Linen and silk were popular fabrics. Women wore beautifully embroidered jackets. Even small girls wore makeup. Their faces were painted white with flour. Lips were painted pink. It was very stylish to paint a small red stripe between the eyes and to color the temples green, black, or blue. Chinese women kept their hair braided.

In Japan, the kimono (kee-MOE-noh) was a common garment for all classes of people. Rich people had kimonos made of silk or linen and poor people used calico,

A Japanese woman in a kimono.

a cheap fabric. Later on in the nineteenth century, Japanese woman shaved their eyebrows and blackened their teeth to show they were married.

Hindus and Buddhists always wore draped clothing. They did this for reasons of religion. Clothes that were draped over the body were the oldest and most widespread

30

Many Indian women still wear the sari.

way of dressing. People of ancient India wore the dhoti (DOE-tee), which they wrapped separately around each leg and looked like a pair of baggy pants.

The sari (SAH-ree) is a long piece of cloth that is often framed on three sides with artistic designs of flowering plants and abstract symbols. The word *sari* comes from the Sanskrit word "sate," which means "strip of cloth."

Fabric that is not sewn is important in the Indian culture. Such a fabric is believed to be pure and graceful because no needle has touched it. It is gently wrapped and draped over the body.

In many cultures, colors have special meaning, and their use in clothing depends on where a person lives. Red is a favorite color in China because it is thought to be lucky. But in Ghana, red is the color of funerals. And in Benin, Africa, red is the color of military power.

In places like the Arab world and India, many people still dress the same way they did in centuries past. Even today millions of people dress like their ancestors did in the Middle Ages.

Chapter 6

The Farthingale: Shape Changer of the Middle Ages

In the late fifteenth century in Spain, the farthingale (FAR-then-gale) was the style of women's clothing. It was made to hold out the skirt around the waist, using hoops of wood, wire, or whalebone. Queen Juana of Portugal is credited—or blamed—for inventing the first stiff underskirt made to drastically change a woman's shape under her clothing. Linen petticoats with circular bands of steel or whalebone became popular all over Spain and Portugal. Women who wore them could not sit down on a chair. They had to sit on pillows piled up on the floor.

The farthingale made a woman's shape grow from hip to hem because the hoops were wider at the bottom. It gave her a bell or dome shape. Eventually, the

Farthingales were sometimes quite large.

farthingale was padded around the hips with something called a bum roll.

The top of the farthingale would be put on a woman's waist to hold out the skirt sideways and then allow it to fall straight down to the floor. Over the farthingale, a woman wore petticoats and a skirt. The

English farthingale was tilted up in the back, giving a woman wearing it an unbalanced look, as if she were about to fall forward. When worn with a corset, the farthingale made a woman look pyramid shaped. Some huge farthingales stuck out from the waist like the spokes of a wheel.

A woman's natural shape was totally hidden when she was wearing a farthingale. Walking, sitting, or even standing was difficult. It was uncomfortable and strange, but no well-dressed woman would go without one.

Chapter 7

The Sixteenth and Seventeenth Centuries
(1500–1699)

en.wikipedia.org

Wigs in the sixteenth and seventeenth centuries were often very elaborate.

In the sixteenth century in Europe, the periwig for men became stylish. The periwig was a close-fitting silk cap with strands of hair sewn into it. Each strand was sewn in one at a time and knotted onto the

36

cap. Wigmakers used goat or horsehair and sometimes even human hair. These wigs were heavy and uncomfortable.

Some men shaved their head bald to make wearing a periwig easier. One story says that Louis XIV (king of France from 1643 to 1715) spread the use of wigs because he had to wear one to cover his own bald spots. Some periwigs were enormous things made of muslin, lace, and ribbons. Tall wigs stood as much as 8 inches above the top of the head.

Most men powdered their wigs with flour or a white clay to make them white. A man had to use a pound or more of flour a week to keep his wig white. Men began putting perfume in the wigs and even coloring them blue.

Other fashions in the sixteenth century were unusual as well. Some men had a single lock of their hair curled so it hung over one shoulder down to the chest. This was called a lovelock. Moustaches and beards became popular and had many

Though strange by our Standards, Louis XIV's clothes in this picture were the height of fashion in his time.

en.wikipedia.org

styles. Facial hair was often stiffened with wax, powdered, and perfumed. Men used curling irons to shape them. Dyeing the hair red was popular.

Spanish stockings were like tights and were a popular style of leg wear for men. Some men also wore striped stockings. In some cases the right leg had black stripes while the left leg had red stripes. Along with their tight stockings, men wore high-heeled shoes. King Louis XIV's outfits, with his long and curly wig, his thigh-high stockinged legs, and his elegant cape, were a good example of this style of men's fashion.

Chapter 8

The Eighteenth Century (1700–1799)

Women's hairstyles grew even stranger and bigger. By the late 1700s, women's hair was piled amazingly high. Women put huge padded wire foundations on their heads to give their hair even more height. In the front they put bunches of fancy curls. The hairdo was held in place with a gel-like substance.

The framework for these hairstyles was so high that the wearer's head and hair was two-thirds the height of her body. The doorway to St. Paul's Cathedral in London, England, was raised four feet so women could walk through the door to worship without knocking over their towering hair.

Inside the framework, the hair was gathered, combed, curled, sprinkled with white powder, and lacquered. Sometimes miniature gardens or model ships were built right into the hairdo. One hairdo

A fashionable woman of the 18th century paid a great deal of attention to her hair.

was designed to remember a battle at sea. Because these hairdos were so complicated, they had to remain in place for a long time. The gardens or model ships could be removed, but the framework remained. The huge framework, which was sometimes as much as 3 feet high, was removed only about once a month, so the woman could wash her hair. Because the hair wasn't kept clean enough, bugs began to live inside the hairdo during the long periods of time when the framework was in place. Some women made slits in the sides of their hairdos so that the bugs could get out. Head lice were common when these huge hairdos were popular.

Hairstyles became so much work that some women began wearing wigs instead. Some women who did not choose one of these huge hairstyles did other things to make their hairstyles pretty. They wove pearls and ribbons through their hair. They dyed their hair blond or gold. In France, women crushed flowers into a powder and dusted their hair with it.

Chapter 9

The Corset: Discomfort Through the Ages

Corsets have a long history and have been around for thousands of years. Among all the bizarre fashions throughout the ages, probably none has caused quite as much discomfort as the corset.

About 4,000 years ago, Minoans of ancient Crete used fitted and laced garments to make their bodies slimmer. Boys also wanted smaller waists, so they would wear corsets, too. Pictures of women wearing corsets were found on ancient coins from Egypt, Rome, Greece, and Assyria (uh-SEER-ee-uh). Greek women wore bands around their waists. Roman women made their slave women wear tight corsets to show their lower status, while the Roman women wore loosely draped clothing.

Evidence showing women wearing an

upper-body garment made from animal skins and laced in the front was found by an archeologist (ark-ee-AHL-uh-jist) in Norfolk, England. He believed that the fresh-killed animal skins were tied to the women's bodies with the tendons of birds and animals. The skins were soft when they were first put on, but as they hardened, they shaped a woman's body into what the people of that time thought of as a more attractive figure.

In Europe during the Middle Ages, stiffer fabrics were used for corsets. Around the sixteenth century, rigid artificial supports were built into the corsets. Ladies-in-waiting had to shrink their waists to no more than thirteen inches around. The steel and iron supports built into the corsets forced their bodies into these tiny shapes.

During the eighteenth century, doctors became concerned that wearing corsets could damage the body. Strangely enough, it was a doctor in the French army who invented something which made corset wearing even more harmful. He designed the metallic eyelet—like we have on our shoes and boots today—which made it possible to lace the corset even tighter without damaging the fabric. The goal was to have a very small waist known as a "wasp waist." This was considered fashionable and attractive.

Colonial women in America were big and muscular. They worked very hard all day and didn't worry much about fashion. But by the nineteenth century in the United States, people's idea of the ideal woman had changed. A woman was supposed to be a pale, fragile creature who had a tiny waist and fainted a lot. So the corset became even more popular from the early 1800s up to the early 1900s.

While wearing the tight corsets, some women suffered dislocated kidneys, livers, and other organs. Frequent fainting spells were common among women of the 1800s, and much of it was because the corsets were so tight. But fainting spells were considered a desirable female feature. In charm schools,

Women often needed someone to help them into a corset.

girls were taught to faint and look beautiful at the same time.

Corsets were made out of wood, iron, leather, perforated steel, and fabric. They were designed to flatten the stomach and to make the figure more attractive under clothing. Women often had help in lacing themselves into corsets.

Chapter 10

The Nineteenth Century (1800–1899)

A woman wearing a bustle.

Along with the corset went the bustle, which was a crescent-shaped pad made of horsehair that was fitted to the back of the waist and tied on with tapes at the front. The well-dressed woman of the 1800s had a tiny waist, a rear end that stuck out behind her because of the bustle, and pointy high-heeled shoes.

The Victorian period began in the 1860s. In this time a woman had to wear about seven pounds of under-clothing to be well dressed. Ten petticoats, a hoop skirt, and a huge dress decorated with ribbons, flowers, feathers, and beads often added up to as much as thirty pounds. Because her clothing was so heavy and hard to move in, Victorian ladies were told to take tiny steps when walking and to never try to run.

Back in the mid-1700s, women's shoes had pointed toes, buckles, and heels that were about one-and-a-half inches high. But by the 1890s, heels were higher than two inches and much thinner. Although these shoes were very stylish and popular, they were not at all comfortable or healthy.

Wearing very high heels can damage a person's posture, cause falling injuries, and change the shape of the feet. Modern studies have linked the wearing of very high heels to a greater risk for knee and bone damage.

In the nineteenth century, men wore long-tailed coats, such as the kind we see Abraham Lincoln wearing in his photos. The high top hat, or stovepipe hat, was popular. Low-crowned hats were called wide-awakes because of their wide brims. Also popular were Homburg hats, which were soft and flexible.

en.wikipedia.org

Hairstyles for men changed as well. They stopped wearing wigs and wore their own hair short. Only artistic people and musicians had long hair. Men often put waves in *Two 19th century dandies* their short hair and grew moustaches and beards. Large moustaches were quite popular.

Men wanted to have broad shoulders, so pads were sewn into their clothing. Men who dressed very fashionably at this time were called dandies. They wore long frock coats with wide lapels and tight, close-fitting pants with straps that went under their shoes to keep them in place.

Women continued to wear long dresses, often with large puffy sleeves and bigger bustles in the late 1800s. The bustle made a

Bathing suits were quite big in the 19th century.

woman's rear end stick out. People said it looked like a snail carrying its shell behind it. Underskirts, now called crinolines (KRIN-uh-linz), were made of stiff fabric and steel and gave women an hourglass shape—large chest, tiny waist, and large rear end.

Bathing suits at this time were usually short-sleeved, long tunics that were tied with a sash around the waist and worn over ankle-length undergarments that people called drawers.

In the late 1800s, many hairstyles came from France. They ranged from short hair curled into ringlets to turbanlike styles decorated with feathers. It was popular to have veils that hung over the face. Pearl-colored powder gave a woman the desired pale-skin look.

As the nineteenth century ended, no one knew what great changes in fashion were just ahead. Women were about to look as they had never looked before. A clothing revolution would explode in the early 1920s after World War I.

Chapter 11

The Twentieth Century (1900–1999)

The floor-length dresses that had been popular in earlier centuries were no longer in style. Women began wearing dresses that ended at the knee or a bit above. Waistlines on dresses became lower, and the boyish look became popular for women. In beauty shops all over America, long, beautiful curls were cut off. Short, wavy hairstyles were popular. Women liked hats with drooping brims. Makeup included bright red lip color and various shades of eye shadow. As advances in chemistry were made, women had a greater variety of cosmetics to choose from. Lips were shaped into cupid bows, and eyebrows were plucked so that a more attractive line could be drawn on with eyebrow pencils. Eyelids were colored blue for the evening, and lanolin was smeared on to make them shiny.

Women in flapper style

In the 1920s, a style known as the flapper look became very popular for women. It included wearing short, shimmering dresses with V-shaped necklines. The actual word *flapper*, which came to symbolize the rebellious young women of the time, came from wearing unbuttoned galoshes, or boots, which flapped when a girl wearing them walked.

For men, the suit, which today's men wear all the time, became popular. Today's modern look for men actually began in the 1920s.

The flapper look of the 1920s quickly disappeared and dresses became longer in the 1930s. Hemlines went back to being longer, and straight skirts and simpler styles were popular. The average woman's outfit—dress, slip, girdle, shoes, and hat—weighed less than one-and-a-half pounds. It was a time of the Great Depression. People didn't have much money, and they were not very concerned with being in style or wearing the latest fashion.

During the years of World War II in the late 1930s and early 1940s, everything was in short supply, so some clothing items became hard to find. The U.S. government said that fabrics had to be saved as much as possible, so men's suits were made with no cuffs, pleats, or patch pockets. Women's dresses were shorter and had no ruffles. The pencil skirt—a very straight style—only needed the smallest amount of fabric, so it became the most common item of clothing for women. Nylon stockings, introduced in the 1930s, were no longer available, so women in the United States and other countries colored their legs to make it look like they were wearing nylons.

After the war, in the 1950s, the clothes that teenagers wore became important for the first time in history. Before this, boys and girls dressed just the way adult men and women did. But starting in the late 1940s, a special style of clothing was worn just by teenagers. Girls pulled their hair back into ponytails and wore blue jeans rolled up to the knees. Or they wore bobby socks and saddle shoes with big wide skirts over many petticoats. Often these big skirts had felt poodles sewn on them. Both American and

British teenagers began to dress like the celebrities they admired.

Elvis Presley was a very popular rock-and-roll singer in the 1950s. Soon teenaged boys were trying to look like Presley. British teenagers were dressing like their favorite musicians, wearing long overcoats and skinny ties. Other teenagers dressed like the rebellious motorcycle rider played by movie star Marlon Brando.

The 1960s brought many changes in the way young people in the Western world behaved and dressed. To the shock and even outrage of the adults, young men grew their hair very long. Even though men had long hair during past centuries, the sight of hair hanging down to the shoulders of many young men in the 1960s annoyed, angered, and alarmed many people. Young women began wearing very short skirts, called miniskirts. Both young men and women wore T-shirts with political slogans on them, and they wore buttons that proclaimed peace and love.

By 1965, teenagers were setting the major fashion trends, and manufacturers listened to them. Teenagers were only 11 percent of the population of the United States, but teenaged girls bought 20 percent of all the clothing made and also 23 percent of all the makeup sold. Stores began setting up entire departments just for the teenage market. Trendy new stores that sold clothing and accessories only for young people became popular.

The popular fashions of the 1960s may have just been for the young then, but many continued to wear these same styles right into the twenty-first century.

Chapter 12

Everything Old Is New Again

The independent and free spirit of the 1960s led to a variety of styles, including the yuppie (which stands for "young upwardly mobile professionals") look. In the business world today, men and women dress alike. Both often wear blue or black suits. Women might wear pants or slim skirts with hems just below the knee. White blouses without frills resemble the white shirts men wear with their suits. Women wear low-heeled shoes and less makeup than they used to. Their short, neat hair is well styled.

In the twenty-first century, the most important fashion statement is that there is no fashion statement that applies to everyone. Baggy running shorts and faded jeans are worn by all generations. Strange styles come and go, such as the oversized overalls, jeans worn low, and bare midriffs popular with teenaged girls. Tattered and faded jeans are sold at high prices.

Beauty is truly in the eye of the beholder and the fashions of today will soon look silly when they are replaced by what we are told is new. However, most things aren't really new. Many styles that become popular have been borrowed from times past. Today's low-rise jeans are yesterday's hip-huggers. Platform shoes from the 1960s have returned to shoe stores of the 21st century. Today, a teenaged boy's baggy pants look like they are sliding down his body, much like Louis XIV of France more than two hundred years ago when he let his underclothing hang out above his stockings. New styles are really old styles all over again.

Bibliography

Kemper, Rachel H. *Costume.* New York: Newsweek Books, 1977.

Nunn, Joan. *Fashion in Costume, 1200–2000.* 2d ed. Chicago: New Amsterdam Books, 2000.

Racinet, Albert. *The Historical Encyclopedia of Costumes.* New York: Facts on File, 1988.

Schnurnberger, Lynn. *Let There Be Clothes: 40,000 Years of Fashion.* New York: Thomas Learning, 1995.

Sensier, Danielle. *Costumes.* New York: Thomson Learning, 1995.

Sichel, Marion. *History of Men's Costume.* London: Batsford Academic and Educational, 1984.

Sichel, Marion. *History of Women's Costume.* London: Batsford Academic and Educational, 1984.